Learning to Play is Playing to Learn

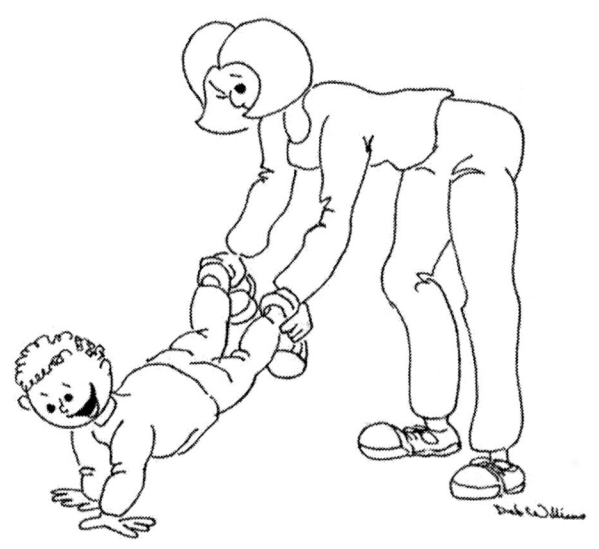

Rosetta Howard

With illustrations by Deborah Williams

Copyright © 2006 by Rosetta Howard
First Edition 2006

Learning to Play is Playing to Learn
by Rosetta Howard

Printed in the United States of America

ISBN 1-60034-608-1

All rights reserved solely by the author. The author guarantees all contents are original and do not infringe upon the legal rights of any other person or work. No part of this book may be reproduced in any form without the permission of the author. The views expressed in this book are not necessarily those of the publisher.

The author guarantees all contents are original and do not infringe upon the legal rights of any other person or work.

www.xulonpress.com

Acknowledgments

The vision for this book is from the seed of God, the Father of our Lord Jesus Christ.

Furthermore, I extend loving acknowledgements to:

> my incredible mother Marilyn and son Donovan, whom God has allowed to be in my life to keep me rooted on my many journeys;
>
> my sister, Patricia Allen, for her endless support in seeing the vision, who is now celebrating her wings in a better place;
>
> Deborah Williams for her creative illustration designs and her "flexibility" to my changes;
>
> in loving memory of Bishop Jack Wallace for cultivating the inspirational seed for my ideas;
>
> and to my current spiritual parents, Pastors Ben and Charisse Gibert, and the Detroit World Outreach Church family for standing in agreement.

Prologue

As the parent of a child born four months early, I learned the importance of child development very early. My relationship with my son is an endless learning chain of questions and patience, which have educated me on what it takes to be his first and most influential teacher.

The more involved I became in his development the more I was able to assist in addressing his styles of learning. Time after time his therapists and schoolteachers commented on how they appreciated the activities and exercises I provided my son to augment his learning capabilities They believed in application principles, and I had a wealth of applied experiences.

I never felt any barrier of intrusiveness and all my applied experiences were welcomed. But I was asked one question phrased in different ways, "A*re you a teacher."*

I would smile and say, *"Yes, his First."* Teaching and learning are not mysteries that can only happen in school.

As parents, you are the principal architect of your children's learning and every family is their first school. So give yourself a big hug for taking on this position where the pay is next to nothing, but the rewards are great.

I hope that this book will help to enhance and strengthen your experiences with your child because **"Every event is a learning stage."**

Rosetta Howard

Introduction

This book emphasizes how "parents or caregivers" are vitally important in being your child's first impressionable "teacher," and how you can use simple items to encourage your child's successful development in language, motor skills and cognitive thinking.

These techniques can assist in building a strong foundation to encourage your child to become an enthusiastic learner throughout his or her early years and beyond.

This book provides everyday "parenting strategies" that will allow your child to be a creative explorer.

"Learning to Play and Playing to Learn" is intended to serve as a warm and delightful book, written in parent-to-parent style that features close-to-home humor with helpful information in practical parenting strategies.

Table of Contents

	Page
Acknowledgements	3
Prologue	4
Introduction	5

Section 1. Parents are Teachers, Too!   9
1. Learning Inspires Play 11

2. How Does Your Child Learn? 15

3. Understanding Domains 19

Section 2. Activities   23
4. Preparations 24

5. Fine Motor Skills 27

6. Gross Motor Skills 63

7. Cognitive Skills 91

Section 3. Epilogue   115
8. It's All About Your Child 117

Section 1

Parents are Teachers, Too!

Section 1. Parents are Teachers, Too!

Chapter 1.
Learning Inspires Play

Section 1. Parents are Teachers, Too!

Chapter 1. Learning Inspires Play

Everyone who interacts with a young child is a teacher. Parents are children's first and most important teachers. This book is written for you with ideas that I learned while raising my preemie son that enhanced his learning development.

This book provides several home-based activities that can promote healthy child development. After the pages of activities, you will also find blank pages which you can use to record your experiences or which can be used to inspire your own ideas as a contribution for your family styles and skill levels.

The years from birth through age five provide an opportunity to break ground and construct the foundation upon which successful lives are built. It is within these years that children develop the basic knowledge, understandings and interests they need to reach the goal of being successful learners, readers and writers.

You play an important role in ensuring growth and change. You spend many hours with your child, and the right kind of activities can help her in tremendous ways to reach success. Often the challenge is teaching the child **"HOW"** to think and **"NOT WHAT"** to think, *which is important.*

The contents of this book are derived from my personal experiences; and, as parents, we all need a *little* help. This is parent-to-parent information that I hope will inspire you to learn-to-play and play-to-learn with your little one.

In order to teach your little one well, *you must be:*
    "Part Clown"
    "Part Actor"
    "Part Friend"

but always the *"PARENT"* with that important responsibility to educate and nurture his young minds.

Always remember that every event is a teachable moment.

Whether you are at home, out shopping or visiting family or friends, take that time to explore, listen and talk with your children.

Before approaching any of the activities in this book, you may wish to discuss them with all concerned persons that have any significant interaction in your child's development. These activities should be conducted with adult supervision so that no harm comes to your precious little person.

When reviewing the activities in this book you will notice that I did not designate any age range. Each child develops at a different level, so use your better judgment based on your child's needs. My son enjoyed many of the activities in this book at a very young age. But he was able to participate with a cognitive understanding when he was around five years of age. Select the activities that are comfortable for you and your family.

As you interact with your child, remember to share control with her, focus on her strengths and support her ideas. If your child wants to paint a stick, support that idea and take the activity outdoors so you can enjoy the sunshine and...also protect your walls.

As a parent, of course, you are responsible for controlling and monitoring your child's activities. But at the same time, foster his independence, initiative and growth by respecting his choices and creativity.

For children, learning is fun!

I hope that learning and playing with your children will be fun for you, too.

I welcome you to adapt or modify the activities in ways that are most meaningful for you and your child. You might even want to take photographs to capture all the fun your child will have.

Keep in mind that some activities may require a little more attention due to the messy supplies suggested. So proceed with caution as you **"Play to Learn."**

Section 1. Parents are Teachers, Too!

Chapter 2.
How Does Your Child Learn?

Section 1. Parents are Teachers, Too!

Chapter 2. How Does Your Child Learn?

Children have two resources for learning:

IMAGINATION and CURIOSITY

As their first teacher, you can awaken your children to the joy of learning by encouraging their imagination and curiosity through "PLAY."

Research in child development has determined that physical movement is the key to the critical connections needed for optimal brain development.

That's right. Your child learns through a series of "PLAY" activities. When you have a child, you must revert to your youth and do some constructive or purposeful play.

The benefits of play can work wonders to promote social skills in children to help them:

- Get along with others
- Learn to take turns and share
- Develop a sense of confidence in their abilities

The physical benefits of play help to:

- Develop balance and build strength to improve muscle control

The intellectual benefits of play help to:

- Develop memory
- Assist in developing problem-solving skills

Learning is easier for everyone involved when children are happy and enjoy what they are doing.

Your job, as their principal architect, is to orchestrate those playful and purposeful experiences. When the activity or toy provides a multi-sensory experience through repetitive actions, learning is taking place.

Children learn by using all of their senses:

- Hearing-touching-tasting-seeing
- Also, playing with objects or manipulations

Section 1. Parents are Teachers, Too!

Chapter 3.
Understanding Domains

Section 1. Parents are Teachers, Too!

Chapter 3. Understanding Domains

How should you select the best activities to enhance your child's development?

Primarily, there are three basic development skills: language, motor, and cognitive.

This book is organized to help you select the appropriate activities for your child's needs. Also, in addition to your own personal observations, you can make this determination based on the advice of your child's teacher, social worker, therapist or physician.

Language activities involve a "give and take" process, such as being:

- Talked to
- Read to
- Listened to

The more you expose your children to language through reading or everyday conversation – the more they will develop in their language skills.

The motor skills of interest are called "gross" and "fine." To help develop balance that may improve muscle control and strength, motor development is equal to physical activity.

Gross motor activities involve the coordination of the large muscles from activities such as riding a bike, running and walking.

Fine motor activities involve coordination of the smaller muscles such as things performed with your hands, coordinating movement of a small toy, weaving yarn in and out of a pattern hole or even folding socks.

Cognitive understanding refers to thinking skills, understanding concepts and intellectual ability, which allow children to think about people's feelings and situations and have an understanding of the world around them. Cognitive development describes the process that people use for remembering, reasoning, and using judgment.

Now, let's explore some activities to play with your children for their success in learning. In reading this book, think how you can implement an activity program once you develop a workable schedule of different activity for each day, week, and even a month to master the desired level.

Just think, you will have created your first lesson plan, and you will then enter into the first stages of your "teaching world." Let every activity of the day be an enjoyable class session!

Section 2

Activities

Section 2. Activities

Chapter 4.
Preparations

Section 2. Activities

Chapter 4. Preparations

To fulfill the activities in this book, you may find yourself entering into the world of becoming the recycle "Queen or King."

Begin by saving the items listed below to name a few, among others described throughout the book.

Keep these materials on-hand for your child's play time:
- children scissors
- craft glue sticks
- construction paper/confetti
- different colored pipe cleaners
- empty paper towel/toilet paper rolls
- feathers
- old buttons

Start recycling these items:
- cans
- egg cartons
- jars and lids
- milk containers
- newspaper
- hot cereal boxes (great for storing craft items)

Section 2. Activities

Chapter 5.
Fine Motor Skills

Section 2. Activities

Chapter 5. Fine Motor Skills

The activities in this chapter can be used to reinforce, stimulate or strengthen the movement of the small muscles in your child's hands and fingers.

Activities for Fine Motor Skills

Activity 1. PIGGYBANK

The pinching movements in this activity will help to strengthen the finger muscles for your future artist or journalist.

Activity 1. PIGGYBANK

Materials needed
- ✓ Piggybank (or slot bank)
- ✓ Coins of different sizes (real or play)

Let's Play and Learn
1. Instruct your child to insert the coins into the bank's coin slot. Carefully observe how your child uses his fingers to pick up the coins.
2. Help him to use only his thumb and index finger, if he can. The pinching movement helps to strengthen those finger muscles for holding a pencil or crayon.

Note your child's progress:

_____
_____
_____
_____
_____
_____
_____
_____
_____
_____

Activities for Fine Motor Skills

© copyright 2006

Activity 2. SPONGE

Here's an activity in which your child can have fun playing in the water and learning to count at the same time!

Activity 2. SPONGE

Materials needed
✓ Sponges (or small, thin face towels) Note: You can also use small, kid-friendly sponges of different shapes.
✓ Basin (or kitchen sink or bath tub)

Let's Play and Learn
Preparations: Fill a basin with water.
1. Have your child place the sponges (or face towels) in the water and squeeze them until the water is released from the sponges.
2. Repeat Step 2 and help your child count how many turns and twists it takes to remove the water.

Note your child's progress:

_____
_____
_____
_____
_____
_____
_____
_____
_____
_____

Activities for Fine Motor Skills

Activity 3. PAPER BALL CHALLENGE

This paper ball challenge (fight) is a good activity for those rainy or snowy homebound days.

Activity 3. PAPER BALL CHALLENGE

Materials needed
✓ Several old newspapers

Let's Play and Learn
1. Help your children separate, crush and shape old newspapers into several small balls.
2. Then you hide the balls around the house.
3. Once all the balls are hidden, the game (fight) begins.
4. Each time your children find a ball, they can throw it out of its hiding place.
5. When all of the paper balls are pulled from their hiding places, get each child to hurriedly gather up the balls and give a count of the number of balls they collect. Note: This is also a way of "cleaning up" the mess!
6. The child who gathers up the most balls is announced as the winner.

Note your child's progress:

_____
_____
_____
_____
_____
_____
_____
_____

Activities for Fine Motor Skills

Activity 4. COTTON BALLS

This is a two-part activity. The pinching movements in this combined activity will help to strengthen your child's finger muscles and his ability to position items in small spaces.

Activity 4. COTTON BALLS

Materials needed
- ✓ Several loose cotton balls
- ✓ Shoe box (or bowl)
- ✓ Tongs
- ✓ Ice tray
- ✓ Child-safe plastic clothespins

Let's Play and Learn
1. Instruct your child to use the tongs to pick up the loose cotton balls and place them one-by-one in the box.
2. When this activity is mastered, have your child take the cotton balls from the box using clothespins (the kind that you have to squeeze to open).
3. Place the balls inside the small sections (one ball per section) of the ice tray.

Note your child's progress:

_____
_____
_____
_____
_____
_____
_____
_____

Activities for Fine Motor Skills

Activity 5. DISCOVERY GAME

Remember, every item and every movement is coordinated for a purpose when you are "playing to learn and learning to play."

Activity 5. DISCOVERY GAME

Materials needed
- ✓ Peanut shaped Styrofoam® packaging materials
- ✓ Box
- ✓ Small toys (such as cars, soldiers, small stuffed animals, and toys in "kids meals" from fast-food restaurants)
- ✓ Timer (or hourglass)

Let's Play and Learn
Preparations: Place the toys inside the box. Then spread the Styrofoam to cover the toys.
1. Have your child use only one hand to rake through the box to search and find each toy.
2. To make the search more interesting, use a timer (egg timer or hourglass) to test her speed and efficiency.
3. Notice your child's excitement when she beats the clock to find all the hidden treasure (toys).

Note your child's progress:

_____
_____
_____
_____
_____
_____
_____
_____

Activities for Fine Motor Skills

Activity 6. PAINTING

For this activity, cover and protect your work area with newspaper or cloth to avoid unnecessary mess and clean up.

Activity 6. PAINTING

Materials needed
- ✓ Eyedropper
- ✓ Coffee filters
- ✓ Water
- ✓ Washable art paint (in paint trays)
- ✓ Clothespins
- ✓ Clothes hangers

Let's Play and Learn
Preparations: Mix the paint slowly with a few drops of water.
1. Help your child take the eyedropper and fill its tube with a pinch of color from the tray.
2. Instruct the child to squeeze and release the paint into the coffee filter.
3. Repeat the previous steps as often as you like using the same or different colors.
4. After the project is completed, attach clothespins to the filter and attach it to the hanger to dry.

Note your child's progress:

_____
_____
_____
_____
_____
_____
_____

Activities for Fine Motor Skills

Activity 7. FINGER RACE

This is a good activity to play at the dinner table or at restaurant table. Focusing your child's attention on a supervised learning activity when in a restaurant will help to minimize distraction from the enjoyment of other patrons.

Activity 7. FINGER RACE

Materials needed
✓ Objects to mark and serve as the "finish line" (such as salt & pepper shakers, eating utensil, pencil)

Let's Play and Learn
Note: You can play the "finger race game" with your child at the dinner table. However, if you play this activity in a restaurant, it is important to play as quietly as you can so the other patrons can enjoy their meals with minimal distraction.
1. Position your "finish line" with whatever is available on the table or in your purse or bag.
2. Do some finger bending to stretch your two racing fingers (located next to the thumb).
3. Quietly call out: "1-2-3- and away you go."
4. Move the two fingers in a "walking fast" motion to the finish line.
5. The first person to reach the finish line marker is the winner. (Of course, when you play with your child, remember to let him win as much as possible.)

Note your child's progress:

_____

_____

_____

_____

_____

Learning to Play Is Playing to Learn

Activities for Fine Motor Skills

Activity 8. FINGER FACE DESIGNS

Here's another activity that's fun to do while at a restaurant. Paper and pencil (or crayons) are always good to carry with you. Encourage your child to scribble or learn to write her name or draw different shapes (circles, squares, and triangles).

Activity 8. FINGER FACE DESIGNS

Materials needed
- ✓ Plain paper
- ✓ Pencil and/or crayons
- ✓ Coins of different sizes

Let's Play and Learn
1. Take turns tracing each other's hands on the paper.
2. Then draw faces on each fingertip on the paper. (See illustration.)
3. Variation: Put some coins under the plain paper and lightly rub your pencil or crayon over the paper, then watch the imprint appear.

Note your child's progress:

_____
_____
_____
_____
_____
_____
_____

Activities for Fine Motor Skills

Activity 9. WATER TOY

I am NOT an advocate for guns. However, water squirt guns (or similar toys) are excellent tools for helping to strengthen your child's finger movements and ability to focus on a target. A Safety Note: I would strongly suggest that you instruct your child to only point –toy gun or not – at inanimate objects. And, never point at a person or animal.

Activity 9. WATER TOY

Materials needed
- ✓ Water squirt guns (or toys that squirt water)
- ✓ Water
- ✓ "Target" (select an area or object that the water will not damage)

Let's Play and Learn
1. Fill the squirt toy with water.
2. Find a safe, appropriate "target."
3. If necessary, help the child squeeze the toy until he can master the activity on his own.

Note your child's progress:

_____
_____
_____
_____
_____
_____
_____
_____
_____
_____

Activities for Fine Motor Skills

Activity 10. CEREAL DROP

Here's another activity that will help your child master and control his finger movements...and he can eat the cereal and raisins when the activity is completed!

Activity 10. CEREAL DROP

Materials needed
- ✓ Small, clean, empty plastic bottle
- ✓ Cereal (preferably oat cereal with the hole in the center)
- ✓ Raisins
- ✓ Chopstick (requires adult supervision)

Let's Play and Learn
1. Instruct and help your child pick up the cereal pieces and the raisins using his index finger and thumb.
2. Then have him drop the cereal and raisins in the bottle.
3. After dropping all the food in the bottle, your child can eat the food—if it won't spoil his appetite for dinner!
4. Here's an additional step for children six-years-old and above: You can instruct your child to retrieve the oat cereal pieces by inserting a chopstick into the hole of the cereal. This step must be monitored with adult supervision to avoid harm to the child.

Note your child's progress:

_____
_____
_____
_____
_____
_____
_____

Activities for Fine Motor Skills

Activity 11. SOCK FOLDING

This is a good activity for small children to master. They will learn a skill that can be helpful with household chores, as well!

Activity 11. SOCK FOLDING

Materials needed
✓   Several clean, matching socks

Let's Play and Learn
The objective of this activity is to have your child match and fold socks appropriately.
1. There are different ways to fold socks. However, for this particular exercise, I recommend the method where you roll one sock inside the other. This method also requires a lot of focus and finger movement control that can help to build your child's fingering dexterity.
2. In addition to this sock folding activity, teach him to fold small face towels. These activities can be fun to learn and will also help to develop a sense of responsibility in your child's maturity.

Note your child's progress:

_____
_____
_____
_____
_____
_____
_____

Activities for Fine Motor Skills

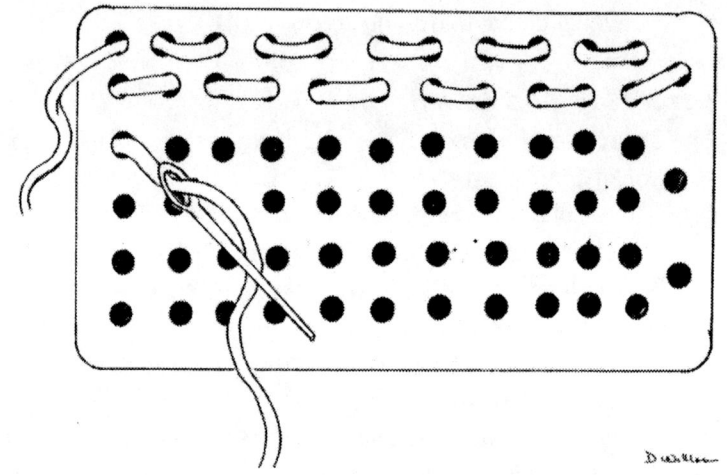

Activity 12. THE WEAVING GAME

This is activity can help your child with eye and hand coordination. Furthermore, this is another activity that can help to keep your child busy while in a restaurant or other public place.

Activity 12. THE WEAVING GAME

Materials needed
- ✓ Loose yarn (or string or ribbon)
- ✓ Hole puncher
- ✓ Cardboard (for example, from inside pantyhose packages)
- ✓ Large knitting needle (optional)

Let's Play and Learn
Preparations: Punch several holes in a piece of cardboard, in any arrangement you desire.
1. Show and help your child to weave the yarn into and out of each hole.
2. For children six-years-old or above, you might show them how to weave the yarn with the use of a knitting needle. Note: This method requires close adult supervision.

Note your child's progress:

_____
_____
_____
_____
_____
_____
_____

Activities for Fine Motor Skills

Activity 13. PAPER TEARING/CUTTING GAME

This is activity can help build and strengthen the muscles in your child's fingers and hands.

Activity 13. PAPER TEARING/CUTTING GAME

Materials needed
✓ Several old newspapers (or magazines)
✓ Small blunt scissors (optional)

Let's Play and Learn
1. Help your child take old newspapers and tear them into ribbon-like strips.
2. If you feel your child is able to handle scissors, show him how to cut out store coupons from the magazines. (It might be wise to start with coupons that you don't wish to redeem—practice makes perfect! After mastering this skill, your child might look forward to cutting out those coupons that you will use at the store! What an accomplishment that will be for him!)

Note your child's progress:

_____
_____
_____
_____
_____
_____
_____
_____

Activities for Fine Motor Skills

Activity 14. FINGER FLICKING

The objective of this activity is to get your child to knock down "standing" crayons with a flicking movement of his thumb and index finger. Very young children may find it difficult to master this motion; they may find it easier to use all four fingers until they are older.

Activity 14. FINGER FLICKING

Materials needed
✓ Crayons, large

Let's Play and Learn
1. Instruct and help your child to get several crayons and stand them up on a table or the floor.
2. Show the child how to position her thumb and index finger in a way that will thump or flick the crayons causing them to fall down.

Note your child's progress:

_____
_____
_____
_____
_____
_____
_____
_____
_____
_____

Section 2. Activities

Chapter 6.
Gross Motor Skills

Section 2. Activities

6. Gross Motor Skills

The activities in this chapter are designed to promote movement and strengthening of the large muscles in the arms or legs. These movements may involve climbing, rolling, jumping or throwing, as well as reaching or carrying objects while mobile.

Activities for Gross Motor Skills

Activity 1. BALL THROWING

You can begin playing ball with your child as soon as your child is able to sit up without support. Playing ball helps to develop hand and eye coordination.

Activity 1. BALL THROWING

Materials needed
Ball (about the size of a softball or slightly larger and made of soft child-safe material, preferably the soft, squeezy type)

Let's Play and Learn
1. Try different types of ball playing games. Start by gently rolling a ball toward him. At first, he may just look at it, but soon he'll try to stop it with his hands and roll it back to you.
2. When you see that your child is mature and strong enough to catch the ball, "then play ball"!
3. Variation: Another game you might try is "2-squares" (Is this telling my age?) or "dodge ball."

Note your child's progress:

_____
_____
_____
_____
_____
_____
_____
_____

Activities for Gross Motor Skills

Activity 2. BOWLING

Recycled items, such as milk cartons, water bottles, or small individual cereal boxes, make great "bowling pins." Don't limit your child's opportunities for having fun as she "learns to play... and plays to learn."

Activity 2. BOWLING

Materials needed
- ✓ Empty milk cartons (or empty water bottles or small empty variety pack cereal boxes)
- ✓ Play sand
- ✓ Soft, small ball

Let's Play and Learn
Preparations: Fill empty milk cartons with a little sand to give them some weight so that the cartons can be used as "bowling pins."

Show your child how to roll her ball toward the cartons (or bowling pins) to knock them all down.

Note your child's progress:

_____
_____
_____
_____
_____
_____
_____
_____
_____
_____

Activities for Gross Motor Skills

Activity 3. SHOEBOX STRETCH

Here's a fun activity where your child can take giant steps!

Activity 3. SHOEBOX STRETCH

Materials needed
Empty shoeboxes (several, maybe 5 or 6)

Let's Play and Learn
Preparations: Place about 5 or 6 empty shoeboxes on the floor throughout the play area.

As shown in the illustration, get your child to walk, taking giant steps, from one box to the next.

Note your child's progress:

_____
_____
_____
_____
_____
_____
_____
_____
_____
_____
_____
_____
_____

Activities for Gross Motor Skills

Activity 4. ANIMAL MIMICKING

Here's an activity where your child gets to draw animal picture/name cards and then mimic animal sounds and behaviors. This is a good learning experience for children.

Activity 4. ANIMAL MIMICKING

Materials needed
3x5 inch index cards (at least six cards)

Let's Play and Learn
1. Help your child use the index cards to draw different animals. Draw one animal per card. Also include the name of the type of animal along with the picture.
2. After your child has drawn the pictures, let him select one card at a time. Then, join your child in mimicking and pretending to be different animals.
3. Be sure to use animal sounds and adapt your child's body to that of the appropriate animal.
4. Below are some suggestions on how to re-create some animals (or use your best interpretation.) For example:
   - *Rabbit Hop.* Position your child to hop around the play area like a rabbit.
   - *Kangaroo.* Tuck your arms in a little and hop around the house.
   - *Snake.* Slide from side to side on the floor. You might also "roll and sliver" on the floor.
   - *Ape.* Beat your chest and make monkey-like gestures, moving your arms under your shoulders.
   - *Giraffe.* Move your neck up and down.
   - *Elephant.* Put your hands under your chin and move them forward in a scooping motion (like tusks).

Note your child's progress:

_____

_____

Activities for Gross Motor Skills

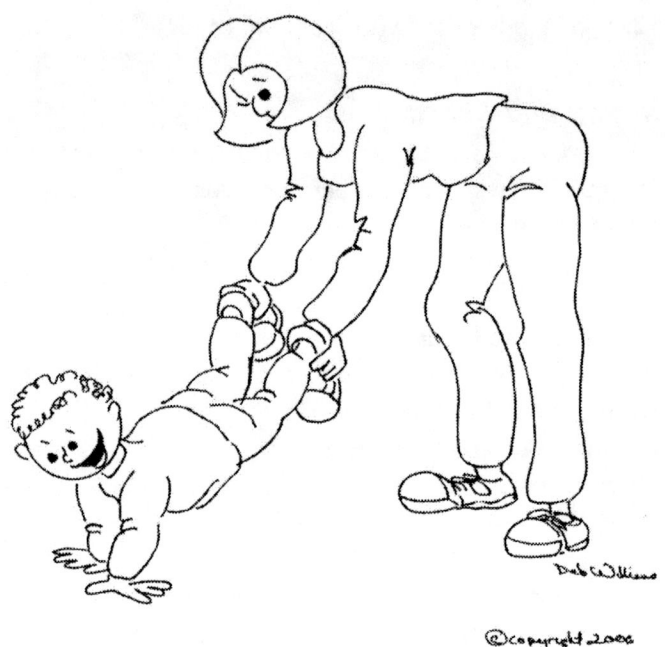

Activity 5. WHEELBARROW

This activity may bring back memories of your own childhood when you walked on your hands and someone was walking behind you holding your feet in the air.

Activity 5. WHEELBARROW

Materials needed
None

Let's Play and Learn
1. Securely hold your child's legs and feet, while he walks on his hands. (See the illustration.)
2. If you have more children and adults (or older children) available, you might form teams of two and have a wheelbarrow race.

Note your child's progress:

_____
_____
_____
_____
_____
_____
_____
_____
_____
_____
_____
_____

Activities for Gross Motor Skills

Activity 6. STAIR STRETCH

If you have stairs in your house, this is a great exercise. Furthermore, this activity can help in teaching your child to count by one's and two's for her future math homework.

Activity 6. STAIR STRETCH

Materials needed
Stairs

Let's Play and Learn
This exercise also helps to stretch those large muscles while learning to play. This activity should be done with adult supervision.
1. Take turns with your child hopping or stretching up and down the stairs.
2. Then try going up the stairs. Begin by leaping by a count of "one." Then move up to a count of "two" while jumping two stairs at a time.

Note your child's progress:

_____
_____
_____
_____
_____
_____
_____
_____
_____

Activities for Gross Motor Skills

Activity 7. SINGING AND DANCING

Music can be a lot of fun. Music is also very powerful. It's a great way of motivating your child to do various exercises. Furthermore, music and song can help to facilitate ways of getting your child to help around the house!

Activity 7. SINGING AND DANCING

Materials needed
Compact disc (CD) or audio tape with nursery school-type music; or songs with age-appropriate content by popular artists (optional)

Let's Play and Learn
This activity will help your child with language development and get him prepared to do age-appropriate household chores. Make sure you're really having FUN!

1. You can make up your own lyrics. Here's a song you can try:
   This is the way we pick up our toys,
   Pick up our toys, Pick up our toys
   This is the way we pick up our toys
   When we are finished playing.
2. The same idea can apply to washing dishes, cleaning his bedroom, brushing his teeth, combing his hair, etc.

Note your child's progress:

_____

_____

_____

_____

_____

_____

Activities for Gross Motor Skills

Activity 8. BEDROOM WALK

This activity involves walking with rhythm! It's also a great way to get your child ready for bed.

Activity 8. BEDROOM WALK

Materials needed
None

Let's Play and Learn
This activity takes imagination and good feet! Here are some ideas to get him ready for bed:
> Join your child in skipping, hopping, crawling backward, marching like soldiers or doing a "heel-toe" movement toward the bedroom.

Note your child's progress:

_____
_____
_____
_____
_____
_____
_____
_____
_____
_____
_____
_____

Activities for Gross Motor Skills

Activity 9. "BACKWARD DAY" GAME

All activities are performed "backwards," including walking, and going up or down stairs. Of course, going up the stairs backwards works best with handrails! This activity will help to strengthen your child's concentration and leg muscles. Note: Monitor your child closely to avoid any bodily harm.

Activity 9. "BACKWARD DAY" GAME

Materials needed
A variety of possible items (See instructions below.)

Let's Play and Learn
This activity can be used in a variety of different ways. You could have your child put on his shirt backwards, walk backwards, climb the stairs backwards, etc.

Note your child's progress:

_____
_____
_____
_____
_____
_____
_____
_____
_____
_____
_____
_____

Activities for Gross Motor Skills

Activity 10. SCAVENGER HUNT

Here's a great activity. Have fun walking with your child around the neighborhood and observing nature together. It's a great way to get your child to move and exercise his muscles, and you can encourage conversation with him to aid in his language development.

Activity 10. SCAVENGER HUNT

Materials needed
- ✓ Paper
- ✓ Pencil or pen

Let's Play and Learn
Preparations: This activity takes place in the great outdoors! Dress appropriately for the weather.
1. Take along some paper and pencil.
2. Get your child to identify different objects, animals, buildings, etc., that he sees along the trail.
3. You can also create a list of items prior to walking and check them off as you come upon them.
4. Your observation list might include: Different animals, such as rabbits, dogs, cats, ducks, squirrels. You might also note flowers, traffic lights, stop signs, flags, police cars, fire trucks, different types of stores and businesses, etc.

Note your child's progress:

_____
_____
_____
_____
_____
_____
_____

Activities for Gross Motor Skills

Activity 11. RING AROUND THE PENCILS

Here's an outdoor activity. Remember, adult supervision is required.

Activity 11. RING AROUND THE PENCILS

Materials needed
- ✓ Pencils (or rulers)
- ✓ Rubber bands
- ✓ Sand

Let's Play and Learn
Preparations: This is an outdoor activity. Note: This activity requires adult supervision.
1. Hide an odd number of rubber bands in a mound of sand or in a sandbox.
2. Both you and your child will each take a pencil.
3. Both of you will kneel by the pile of sand.
4. Get your child to say "Go" as a signal for each of you to begin plunging your pencils into the sand to uncover and pick up the rubber bands with the pencils.
5. When all the rubber bands have been uncovered, the person with the most on his pencil wins.

Note your child's progress:

_____
_____
_____
_____
_____
_____

Section 2. Activities

Chapter 7.
Cognitive Skills

Section 2. Activities

7. Cognitive Skills

The activities in this chapter can be used to stimulate and strengthen cognitive development and personal confidence in your child.

Children need to have opportunities to experience their own successes, solve problems, ask questions, and use words to describe their ideas, observations and feelings.

These exercises utilize various methods and toys to reinforce exploration, sequencing, symbol recognition, memory, attention, concentration, problem-solving and decision-making.

Activities for Cognitive Skills

Activity 1. UPSIDE-DOWN READING

Here's a cognitive test you can administer to your child. See if she will notice that you're trying to read from a book when it's held upside down. See if she can "pass the test." Furthermore, if she does notice the error, she will love "correcting your mistake"!

Activity 1. UPSIDE-DOWN READING

Materials needed
Children's reading book

Let's Play and Learn
1. This time, when you begin your reading session with your child, hold the book upside down.
2. Notice whether your child will announce that the text and pictures in the book are being held in the wrong direction.
3. Here's a suggestion: Then say, "I was wondering why the picture and words look different."
4. Then place the book in the proper position and read the story.
5. Ask your child questions about the content of the story to determine whether he understands it. (Questions beginning with "who…," "what…," "when…," "where…," and "why…" are great ways to form your questions.)
6. Use age-appropriate language to help her express her ideas and understand the concepts in the story.

Note your child's progress:

_____

_____

_____

_____

_____

Activities for Cognitive Skills

Activity 2. BACKWARD

Cognitive exercises are designed to help children identify and solve problems, recognize differences, and deal with situations that require judgment.

Activity 2. BACKWARD

Materials needed
T-shirt (or pajama top)

Let's Play and Learn
1. When you help your child get dressed, make a deliberate effort to turn his T-shirt inside out.
2. Notice whether he indicates that the shirt is applied the wrong way.
3. Make this a fun activity where he can "correct your mistake!"

Note your child's progress:

Activities for Cognitive Skills

Activity 3. TABLE SETTING

Ask your child questions, such as: How many people are eating dinner tonight? How many spoons do we need? Let's count them. This allows her to count objects correctly, follow simple directions, and accept responsibility

Activity 3. TABLE SETTING

Materials needed
- ✓ Plates
- ✓ Cups
- ✓ Napkins
- ✓ Eating utensils (spoons, forks, table knives)

Let's Play and Learn
Children love learning to take responsibility. This activity will get your child involved with making "adult-type" decisions.
1. Teach her how to count out the number of utensils needed for the meal based on the number of family members or guests that will be present.
2. Teach her how to position the plates, cups, and eating utensils on the table.

Note your child's progress:

_____
_____
_____
_____
_____
_____
_____
_____

Activities for Cognitive Skills

Activity 4. DOT-TO-DOT

This activity can help your child identify crayon colors.

Activity 4. DOT-TO-DOT

Materials needed
- ✓ Paper
- ✓ Crayons (one color for each player)

Let's Play and Learn
Preparations: Take a sheet of paper and draw small dots in rows of ten down and across about half-inch apart all over the paper. (See the illustration.)
1. Take alternating turns with your child making one connecting line between two dots that are next to each another.
2. The person who makes the line that forms and completes a "square" can fill in the square with his crayon color.
3. The player with the most squares in his crayon color wins the game.

Variation: Rather than filling in the square with color, fill in the square with the initials of your first and last names.

Note your child's progress:

_____
_____
_____
_____
_____
_____

Activities for Cognitive Skills

Activity 5. IDENTIFYING FAMILY MEMBERS

This activity will help your child exercise her cognitive abilities to identify significant people in her life—especially family and friends...past and present, in town and out of town.

Activity 5. IDENTIFYING FAMILY MEMBERS

Materials needed
- ✓ Photographs of family members
- ✓ Index cards
- ✓ Pencil (or crayon)

Let's Play and Learn
1. Bring out photographs of family members.
2. Write their names on separate index cards.
3. Place all the cards and photos face down.
4. Turn a single photo face up.
5. Help your child identify the person in the photo.
6. Once he identifies the photo correctly, locate the appropriate name card and place it next to that photo.
7. Repeat Steps 4 thru 7 until all the photos are revealed and identified.
8. This exercise can be a great way for your child to learn about relatives and friends.

Note your child's progress:

_____
_____
_____
_____
_____
_____
_____

Activities for Cognitive Skills

Activity 6. ROLE PLAYING

This activity can help the child express his creativity and imagination.

Activity 6. ROLE PLAYING

Materials needed
A children's book with an action-oriented storyline

Let's Play and Learn
1. When reading to your child, take the time to get your child to act out some of the scenes or characters in the story.
2. Find books that will provide your child with vibrant, lively characters. Nursery rhymes are also good because they are rhythmic and easy to remember.

[Author's note: A favorite book for my son was **Caps for Sale** by Esphyr Slobodkina. It was wonderful to role-play the hat salesman and place a lot of hats on our heads. My son and I would take turns playing the hat salesman and the monkey. Eventually, my son knew the storyline and the script without my having to read it to him.]

Activities for Cognitive Skills

Activity 7. PLAYING DICE

This activity can help your child with "number recognition." Playing with dice or playing cards can also help your child develop an understanding of the concepts: "higher than" or "less than," which are extremely important when learning arithmetic.

Activity 7. PLAYING DICE

Materials needed
A pair of dice

Let's Play and Learn
1. Give your child one dice, while you take the other dice.
2. Each player takes his dice and rolls it on the floor or table.
3. After each of you has rolled your dice once each, note that the players with the highest number wins that set.

Variations: Set the game challenge at 50. The first person to get to 50 points is the winner. Another variation would be to substitute the dice with a deck of cards.

Note your child's progress:

_____
_____
_____
_____
_____
_____
_____
_____
_____
_____

Activities for Cognitive Skills

Activity 8. GAME MARATHON

Games help strengthen your child's memory, matching abilities, and logical thinking. Board games and card games require concentration. Memory games can help to increase your child's concentration and strategy planning abilities.

Activity 8. GAME MARATHON

Materials needed
- ✓ Board games (checkers)
- ✓ Playing cards (different types)
- ✓ Tic-tac-toe/hangman (using 2-3 letter words)
- ✓ Bingo®
- ✓ Memory games

Let's Play and Learn
Have a "marathon" evening of various board and table games.
1. Play your own version of checkers without too many rules at first. You want your child to be able to concentrate and plan strategic moves as much as she can handle.
2. Then decide when she is ready for the board game rules. Just focus on one main task at a time.
3. Here is another "out the bag" game: Tic-tac-toe, which can increase concentration and develop strategic skills in planning.
4. Play different card games or create some that suit your family. Try various table games, such as Bingo®. Also introduce memory games, such as Old Maid® card game.

Note your child's progress:

_____

_____

_____

_____

_____

Activities for Cognitive Skills

Activity 9. MUSIC MAKERS

From birth (and perhaps even before that time), music can stimulate your child's brain. Music can also serve as a wonderful platform for developing skills in listening, language and creativity.

Activity 9. MUSIC MAKERS

Materials needed
- ✓ Pots and pans
- ✓ Wooden spoon

Let's Play and Learn
When your child opens that kitchen cabinet door to pull out pots and pans, join in on the fun with a wooden spoon and make sweet rhythmic noises that only a child and parent can appreciate and share together.

Note your child's progress:

_____
_____
_____
_____
_____
_____
_____
_____
_____
_____
_____
_____

Section 3

Epilogue

Section 3. Epilogue

Chapter 8.
It's All About Your Child

Section 3. Epilogue

Chapter 8. It's All About Your Child

Let your child's imagination flourish with ideas that only he or she can construct.

Most importantly, have fun with your child as you "learn to play" and master more skills from the games and activities while you "play to learn."

You have all the essential tools around you to build the practical foundation for learning in your child's world. Furthermore, "exploratory" play helps develops children in all areas of cognitive, language and motor skills. Building their foundation in learning depends on you...and you are so *vitally important* in their journey of development.

Remember to use the blank pages throughout this book for capturing notes on your child's progress or for noting your own individualized ideas for creating additional activities.

I would like to depart with these words:

> *Tell me – and I might forget it.*
> *Teach me – and I might remember it.*
> *Involve me – and I will learn it.*

Happy parenting power to you,

Rosetta

The Author

Rosetta Howard is a facilitator of parenting workshops.

She has worked for several years as a Certified Parent Educator and a Parent Facilitator for many agencies.

She is the mother of a young son, born four months prematurely, whose growth, development and progress have given her years with many opportunities to apply her parenting and practical experiences to the contents of this book.

Howard is also the founder of Parent Group Facilitators. Its objective is to provide tips, tools and guidance to parents on how to effectively understand the "positive" attributes within a family structure that will assist to nurture a healthy, developing child and promote effective family support.

The mission and philosophy of PGF is to foster a strong and practical foundation through effective and positive family fun activities and play.

For more information, contact Rosetta Howard at PGFacilitators@yahoo.com.

Printed in the United States
63555LVS00002B/1-240